The Lamp Maker

Cindy Starr Stewart

Illustrated by Dan Drewes

CrossBooks™
A Division of LifeWay
1663 Liberty Drive
Bloomington, IN 47403
www.crossbooks.com
Phone: 1-866-879-0502

First published by CrossBooks 6/25/2012

ISBN: 978-1-4627-1939-6 (sc)

Printed in the United States of America

This book is printed on acid-free paper.

Any people depicted in stock imagery provided by Thinkstock are models, and
such images are being used for illustrative purposes only.

Certain stock imagery © Thinkstock.

Because of the dynamic nature of the Internet, any web addresses or links contained in this book may have changed
since publication and may no longer be valid. The views expressed in this work are solely those of the author and do
not necessarily reflect the views of the publisher, and the publisher hereby disclaims any responsibility for them.

CROSSBOOKS
PUBLISHING

I would like to thank the Lord for entrusting this story to me and for giving me the opportunity to share it for His glory. Lance, thank you for always encouraging me to trust the Lord and to take giant steps of faith. Noah, Caleb, Libby, Tessa & Judah; I love you all so much and I am proud of each one of you for the way you let His light shine through you. Keep shining!

There is only one Great Lamp Maker
who crafts lamps of every style;
big ones, small ones,
pretty ones and tall ones
and ones that make you smile.

Some lamps are so pretty,
made carefully with little pieces of colored glass,
while others are super stylish
made with craftiness and class.

Some are to brighten basements and
others are a beacon on a hill.
There are lamps for every kind of job,
each one with a purpose to fulfill.

Now you are the body of Christ, and each one of you is a part of it.
1 Corinthians 12:27

The Maker gently creates each lamp
and He does so with such tender love.
Each and every one is unique
and has an assignment from the Master above.

With love and care He fashions
every single lamp just right.
He does so with one purpose in mind.
It is created to shine light.

Yes, light is the main purpose
for which each lamp is made,
light to shine for all to see,
not to be hidden under a shade.

For you created my inmost being; you knit me together in my mother's womb.
Psalm 139:12-14

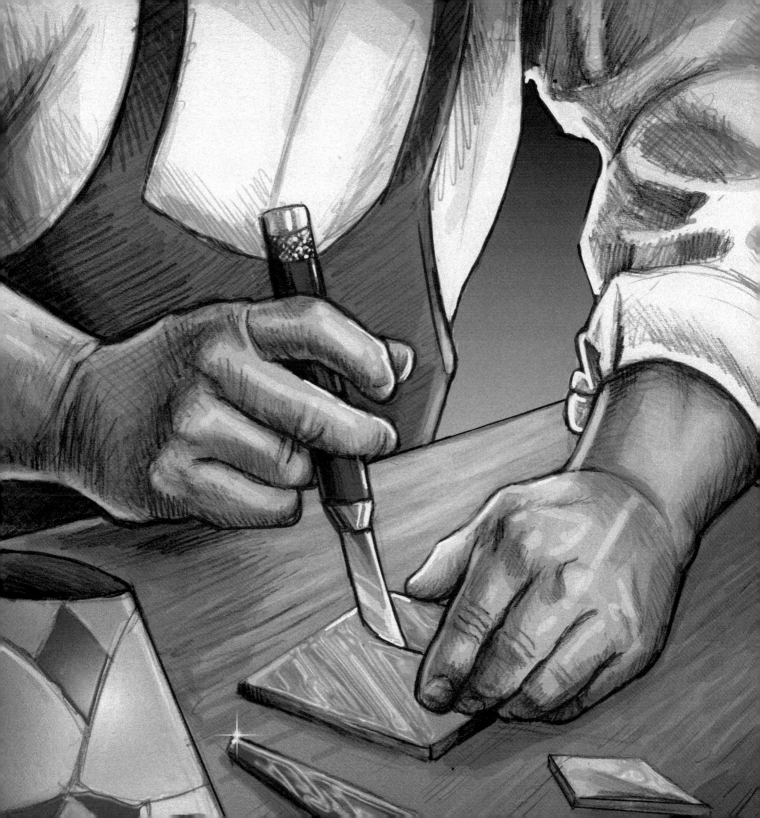

*After each lamp is created,
complete with every part,
it is carefully shipped to the place
where it is ready to make its start.*

*No matter what the lamp,
no matter what the kind,
each lamp is shipped without one thing,
yes one thing is left to find.*

*While each lamp is created carefully
to shine with beams so bright,
every lamp arrives to its new home
without that bulb of light.*

Light has come into the world, but people loved darkness instead of light because their deeds were evil. Everyone who does evil hates the light, and will not come into the light for fear that their deeds will be exposed. But whoever lives by the truth comes into the light, so that it may be seen plainly that what they have done has been done in the sight of God. John 3:19-21

You see a lamp cannot shine light
without a light bulb screwed in.
No matter how hard it tries,
the gleaming just won't begin.

The light will not shine from the lamp
unless a bulb is in place,
and once the bulb is screwed in tight,
it's only the start of the race.

I press on toward the goal to win the prize for which God
has called me heavenward in Christ Jesus.
Philippians 3:14

*Now the lamp needs one more thing
in order for light to shine.
It must be plugged into a source of power
with which it will combine.*

*Everything the lamp needs
for the light to come out right...
a bulb fastened in, then plugged into the socket
surely brings delight.*

But you will receive power when the Holy Spirit comes on you: and you will be my witnesses
in Jerusalem, and in all Judea and Samaria, and to the ends of the earth. Acts 1:8

Delight to each and every one
who sees the magnificent light.
Now everything is coming together.
It is all working out just right.

It's like the Master planned it.
The lamp is shining bright.
A light for all the world to see
even in the darkest night.

Light that shines from each lamp
made in the Master's hand;
brings life, love, joy and peace
to a dark and dreary land.

In him was life, and that life was the light of all mankind. The light shines
in the darkness, and the darkness has not overcome it. John 1:4-5

So here is the big question that you must be asking by now.

"What's this story all about?
Does it relate to me?
How?"

You see the Great Lamp Maker is God
who created you with love.
Your Heavenly Father loves you so much
and crafted you from above.

He knows everything about you
and designed you to shine light
in a dark and scary world
where nothing seems quite right.

"For I know the plans I have for you," declares the Lord, "plans to prosper you and not to harm you, plans to give you a hope and a future." Jeremiah 29:11

He sent His only son Jesus
to pay for your every sin,
to clean you up and make you whole
and to let His light come in.

Jesus said He is the Light and
the Holy Spirit is the power.
If you want His light to shine in you
then let this be the hour.

The true light that gives light to everyone was coming into the world. He was in the world, and though the world was made through him, the world did not recognize him. He came to that which was his own, but his own did not receive him. Yet to all who did receive him, to those who believed in his name, he gave the right to become children of God- children born not of natural descent, nor of human decision or a husband's will, but born of God. John 1:9-13

This is the hour He has called you to,
He wants to come right in;
and fill you up with all His light
and cleanse you from all sin.

And when your sin is all washed away
and your light bulb is in place,
then let the power of His Holy Spirit flow
and watch His beautiful light fill your face.

Your face will shine with light so bright
that all the world will see,
that in you lives the one and only Savior,
Jesus Christ is HE!

For God so loved the world that he gave his one and only Son, that whoever believes in him shall not perish, but have eternal life. For God did not send his Son into the world to condemn the world, but to save the world through him. John 3:16

But what happens when you sin again
and want to do things all your way?
What will happen then to the light?
Will it dim or fade to grey?

You see each day you have free will
and you have the right to choose;
to live for Christ with His light
or live for self and then His light you lose.

If we claim to have fellowship with him and yet walk in the darkness, we lie and do not live out the truth. But if we walk in the light, as he is in the light, we have fellowship with one another, and the blood of Jesus, his Son, purifies us from all sin. 1 John 1:6-7

It does not leave or get burned out,
It just cannot shine bright;
because to have His light shine through you,
you must choose to live life right.

But God, who is rich in mercy, because of the great love he had for us, even when we were dead in our transgressions, brought us to life with Christ, raised us up with him, and seated us with him in the heavens in Christ Jesus, that in the ages to come he might show the immeasurable riches of his grace in his kindness to us in Christ Jesus. For by grace you have been saved through faith, and this is not from you; it is the gift of God; it is not from works, so no one may boast. For we are his handiwork, created in Christ Jesus for the good works that God has prepared in advance, that we should live in them. Ephesians 2:4-10

When you choose each day to trust Him
and put Him first in line,
His light will always shine from you
each and every time.

So thank you to the Lamp Maker,
the Creator up above.
Thank you for sending Jesus
and filling us with love.

Praise and glory belong to Jesus
because He is the one true Light
that fills us up from head to toe
and sets our lives aright!

"Therefore, if your whole body is full of light, and no part of it dark, it will be just as full of light as when a lamp shines its light on you." Luke 11:36

So now that you know that you are a lamp,
are you are wondering,
"Where's my light?"
Just lift your eyes to God above
and receive His Son tonight.

As soon as you pray the words
from deep within your heart,
the Holy Spirit of God fills the void in you
bringing your new life to a start.

Your name will be written in the Book of Life
and from that moment on;
you will know, that you know, that you know, that you know
that your spirit will live on!

The one who is victorious will, like them, be dressed in white. I will never
blot out the name of that person from the book of life, but will acknowledge
that name before my Father and his angels. Revelation 3:5

Now that His Spirit is living in you
and you're plugged into His power,
let your light shine bright my friend,
each and every hour!

Neither do people light a lamp and put it under a bowl. Instead they put it on its stand, and it gives light to everyone in the house. In the same way, let your light shine before others, that they may see your good deeds and glorify your Father in heaven. Matthew 5:15-16

When Jesus spoke again to
the people, he said, "I am
the light of the world.
Whoever follows me will
never walk in darkness, but
will have the light of life."
John 8:12

Dear Lamp Maker,

Thank you for creating me to shine light. I am sorry that I have not been obeying your Word or living my life for you. Thank you for forgiving me of my sins because of what Jesus did for me on the cross. I receive your forgiveness and I forgive myself as well. I know that I cannot shine light without Jesus. Right now, I receive him into my heart and ask that you fill me with his love and his light. I also know that I need to be plugged into the power of the Holy Spirit and so I am giving him permission to flow through all of me every day. Help me to choose to live for Christ and not for my own selfish desires. When I live for self it's like turning off the light switch of my life. But when I die to self and live full of the Spirit, then the light is switched on so that the Lord's light can shine through me. Help me to choose to trust you above all else. I want to live a powerful Spirit-filled life that is pleasing to you so that others will be drawn to your light as well.

Love,